I0413684

# Black Background Adult Coloring Book

## Black Background Mandala Coloring Book For Adults, featuring various Mandala Patterns.

Black Background Adult Coloring Books: Vol 1

by The Coloring Book People

ISBN-13: 978-1535155144

ISBN-10: 1535155140

# COLOR TEST PAGE

# COLOR TEST PAGE

www.ingramcontent.com/pod-product-compliance
Lightning Source LLC
Chambersburg PA
CBHW081125280526
45787CB00007B/2989